GRACE of ANGELS

For Megan, Laura, Rebecca
and the thirteenth Angel

Grace of Angels

GABRIELLE LORD

For Pat,
Happy birthday,
Best wishes (Lib +) Gabrielle
May '96

BANTAM BOOKS
SYDNEY • AUCKLAND • TORONTO • NEW YORK • LONDON

GRACE OF ANGELS

A BANTAM BOOK

First published in Australia and New Zealand
in 1995 by Bantam

National Library of Australia.
Cataloguing-in-Publication Entry

Lord, Gabrielle, 1946–.
Grace of Angels

ISBN 1 86359 731 X

1. Angels. 2. Prayer. 3. Spiritual life. I. Title

291.43

Bantam books are published by

Transworld Publishers (Aust) Pty Limited
15–25 Helles Ave, Moorebank, NSW 2170

Transworld Publishers (NZ) Limited
3 William Pickering Drive, Albany, Auckland

Transworld Publishers (UK) Limited
61–63 Uxbridge Road, Ealing, London W5 5SA

Bantam Doubleday Dell Publishing Group Inc
1540 Broadway, New York, New York 10036

Cover design by Juan Carlos Camacho/Reno Design Group 14660
Cover Illustration by Paul Klee, "Forgetful Angel", 1939
Text design by Juan Carlos Camacho/Reno Design Group 14954
Typeset in 13/20 Cochin by Midland Typesetters
Printed by Australian Print Group

10 9 8 7 6 5 4 3 2 1

Contents

INTRODUCTION

When the publisher first raised the possibility of this book, I hesitated because I'd wanted one day to write a book of 'secular' prayers, especially for women, and angels were not my competence. We'd talked about how it was that many people have been too hurt by childhood 'religious' teachings ever to pray again, despite the fact that there are times in every life when we need prayers so badly. It was she who suggested the combination of prayers and angels.

As she said this, I suddenly realised that angels are user-friendly. No one has bad feelings about angels in the way they might have about notions of God. Then, said the publisher, very wisely, 'It would also give them back their original position—intermediaries between us and the Divine.' That's when I saw it: prayers and angels. In that sense, every prayer bridges the gap ; every prayer is an intermediary; every prayer is an angel until we have each experienced our connection with the Source; in some mysterious way, come home.

I want to make it clear that I have had to throw out everything I was taught concerning goal-oriented prayer and the punishing God of my convent education (I sometimes say I was 'razed' by the nuns, because that was how I experienced my schooling). I had to dismantle—not always fully or successfully, I'm sad to say—the harsh attitudes of my teachers which I had unwittingly taken on, rejecting their words, yet absorbing their bleak attitudes, their black and white thinking, their *a priori* contempt for anything different, anything outside their narrow focus.

This is how I have come to understand that it is attitudes, not information that are passed on in families and also in formal teaching. Any teaching system that objectifies the child into a creature to be trained, indoctrinated or 'improved' into submission and docility, rather than nurtured and supported into individuality, is *abusive at the outset,* and from this unloving state of things, all further forms of abuse are possible, perhaps even inevitable. This is not special pleading, but of relevance to the peace of the world.

Objectified children grow up into objects rather than fully human people, and objects are not capable of loving.

Whatever mistakes we make in attempting to move closer to each other, whatever unskilfulness, however clumsy these attempts are, they are sacred in their intention. Unless you allow yourself to settle into the fact that you're an ordinary person, you can't come into the kingdom of Truth. Until you allow yourself to become ordinary, you might not be able to admit to any of the ordinary things that form part of the human experience. Many of us ordinary folk, especially women, were condemned by a system that had no room for our experience, no acceptance of our different and unique ways of seeing and experiencing life, no respect for our integrity, or the dignity of our suffering.

Only later did we come to see that although these rigid people and their rigid institutions thought they held the truth, they were mistaken in their beliefs. This book is especially for us.

PRAYER TO THE ANGEL OF THE GRAIL

Mysterious vessel, shining in your hands,
container full of grace, protected by your wings
Angel of the Sacred Grail, teach me containment.
Strong containment, supporting all my aspects.
Otherwise, heart seems feeble, cannot bear the depth of life
and eggshell skin explodes through fear or rage or hatred,
lashing out and hurting self and others.
Show to me my vastness, heights and depths.
Expanse of soul worlds, more immense than galaxies.
So much spaciousness, so much room in heart for all of me,
sweet and bitter, lost and found, dark and radiant,
fear and love, letting go and holding on.
In this self is everything, In all selves the same self.
When the alchemy is done
and leaden judgement turned into love's gold,

I come to see immortal truth.
I am the grail that holds the world.
I am the love that shines on all as angels hold me
and I learn the answer to the riddle:
'Whom does the grail serve?'

PART ONE

History of Angels

A TANGLE OF ANGELS

'But where do they come from?' a writer friend asked me when he heard I was doing a book about angels. 'And what are they?' His family is Census-form-only-Protestant, and he has no history of angelic iconography as I have.

They come from everywhere. From the Assyrians, the Persians, the Greeks, the Hebrews, the Romans, from China and from the Middle East. Whatever else they are, angels are certainly not exclusive to Christianity.

According to fourteenth century Jewish cabbalists there are 301 655 722 angels abroad in the world.

A very beautiful angel, termed a 'winged god of luck', the Kairos of Tragir, appears in relief in the third century BCE, tipping a set of scales, and a fifth century BCE Etruscan tomb painting from Tuscany depicts a winged 'demon', tall and sturdy, pinions decoratively fletched as any Fra Angelico was to paint nearly two thousand years later.

During excavations of the palace of King Ahab in Samaria, an ivory carving of a winged being was discovered. This fellow almost exactly coincides with Ezekiel's sixth century BCE description of an angel that he was preaching to the Babylonians:

> *As to the likeness of their faces, they had the face of a man, and they had the appearance of a lion on the right side (of their body) and the appearance of an ox on the left side, and their wings were stretched upward, two wings of every one were joined, one to another, and two covered their bodies. (Ezk 1:10–11)*

Angels are common to all sources of our particular culture. But *what* are they? Leftover spirits from the various pagan otherworlds? Sorts of 'holy fairies'? Creatures of the imagination who exist only in myth and legend like the unicorn? Or are they *energies* in mind surging between the synapses that create thought—the poetic personification of a mysterious mental event?

The word 'angel' comes from the Greek for 'messenger'. In Greek mythology, Hermes with his winged feet and healing wand, mediated often between Olympus and earth. He also ran errands for the Underworld. Hermes, or Mercury to the Romans, had the ability to move freely throughout the three worlds. Loki, from whom we get our modern day word 'lucky', served a similar purpose in the myths of the Nordic people.

In the Judaeo-Christian tradition that forms, among other things, a vague container for our culture of today, angels were always taken seriously as personal beings of self-awareness and power. But there is tremendous variety and difference over the ages in the way that angels are described and taught.

In the pre-Exilic period of Jewish history, angelic doctrine is relatively simple and can be summed up by saying that there are a great many angels, they live near God in heaven and they are sent as messengers. It is not until the post-Exilic period that angelogy really starts to take off. Names and orders of angels are developed and in Daniel, Job and Tobias, angels with personal names appear. The overlapping of spiritual traditions, Jewish, Islamic and Christian, creates influences that must have affected early Christian teaching, and hence our Western understanding of angels. For instance, in the Islamic religion, the Holy Spirit is identified with Gabriel. There is a reflection of this in Christianity's Annunciation story, where it is Gabriel who announces to the young maiden that she is to conceive through the power of the Holy Spirit. In some medieval paintings, the Holy Spirit is seen as a dove emitting a ray of light that enters the body of the maiden through her ear.

Just as there are many different teachings on angels, there is equal confusion about demons. Some early writings reflect the belief that the fallen angels are actually us—human beings. The early Church father Origen argues that the spirits dwelling in human bodies are fallen spirits enclosed in a body as punishment. He has very convincing arguments that this is the case. Origen argues that it would be unworthy of the goodness of God if he created rational beings with unequal abilities. (He seems to have had no trouble believing in the existence of human reason.) Therefore, the inequalities we perceive in human beings result from sins, committed before they were born. To enclose a pure spirit in a body, to limit the limitless in time, space and matter, is to imprison indeed, Origen argues.

Pre-Christian teachings suggest that the fallen angels became demons rather than human. (I must say, when I look at the history of the human race, it is often not clear whether we are dealing with demons or humans.) Enoch's angels lusted after human women and married into the human race. Opposed to this is the esoteric view of this 'fall' as intentional and sacrificial; that these angels were so moved by compassion for our suffering, that they decided to 'fall' so as to 'improve' humanity—in a deed of angelic animal husbandry.

The more generally accepted orthodox theological view is that the angels fell through some character defect and everyone seems in agreement that whatever their nature and origin, angels and demons are older than humans.

The early fathers taught that God was above eternity, with the angels inhabiting a sort of 'lower eternity' and us humans lower still, enclosed in time. Just as the angels formed the mediating messengers between God and humans, the demons are the mediating class between the devil and humans: *Diabolus est Deus inversus*. The reflected shadow of Heaven.

As to the devil and who he is and where he comes from and whether or not he is the same as Satan, or Lucifer, or the old Dragon of the Phoenicians, or the Prince of the World (who may be the false matter-making god of the Gnostics, the Demiurge), all that can be said truly is God only knows. And as God only knows good and how to extend love, it is more than possible that God may not know at all. There are so many conflicting accounts of this, that the devil and demonology is almost as complex as angelogy.

St Paul was not entirely happy about the cult of angels but at the Council of Nicaea in 325, it was decreed that faith in angels was part of the dogma. But shortly afterwards, at Laodicea, the cult of angels was deemed idolatrous. Then in 787, an ecumenical synod established a defined and limited cult of angelic dogmata.

Augustine, 354–430, stated that we knew angels existed through faith, and nearly a century later Thomas Aquinas wrote a lot about the angels. In his Treatise on Angels, from the *Summa Theologiae*, Aquinas describes how angels acquire the bodies they need to appear to humans:

> *Air ... when condensed ... can both be shaped and coloured as appears in the clouds. Even so the angels assume bodies of air, condensing it by Divine power in so far as is needful for forming the assumed body.*

These were the days when non-physical events seemed to be able to be understood in terms of 'scientific' explanations. The Treatise is filled with wonderful philosophical speculations as to whether or not an angel knows himself. The answer is 'yes' but this only after long discussions of Aristotlean notions of form, substance and singulars—concepts that most philosophy students will remember from their undergraduate days. Aquinas asks whether an angel knows another, whether they know material things, whether they know the future, whether they know secret thoughts, whether there can be falsity in the intellect of an angel. Whether there is a 'morning' and an 'evening' knowledge in an angel? ('Morning knowledge' refers to the creation and 'evening knowledge' refers to the praise and celebration of the creator that is naturally drawn out of an angel.) He further asks whether there is an 'irascible and concupiscible appetite' in an angel? That is, can angels experience rage and lust? Whether there is love of choice in the angels, whether an angel loves God or himself more, whether the angel was produced by God from eternity and whether angels were created in happiness and in grace.

After this Aquinas investigates the fall of the angels. How could it have happened, given that angels were created by a God that is entirely and utterly good? Eventually, Aquinas comes up with a solution. He argues that there was an interval between the devil's creation and his fall, and in that fall, the devil exercised his angelic intellect to an evil purpose. I don't know how there can be an 'interval' without time.

His great work, the *Summa Theologiae*, was never entirely finished because about fifteen months before his death a great change came over him while he was saying mass. He stopped writing. 'I can do no more,' he said to his brothers. 'Such things have been revealed to me that all I have written seems as straw and I now await the end of my life.' He went on retreat to the Cistercians and prepared for his last journey. I think he saw the angels.

Between these two dominating theologians in time, came St John Damascene, who lived from *c.* 676–749, and formed the opinion that an angel is 'an ever movable intellectual substance'. (What constituted 'substance' was a matter of great interest to Aristotle.) John Damascene was a widely educated man who was condemned with 'a four-fold anathema' four years after his death, but vindicated by the Council of Nicaea in 787.

Eventually, debate settled down and private devotion to angels became unremarkable. The Catholic Church celebrates the feast of three of the archangels, Michael, Gabriel and Raphael, on 29 September, and there is a general feast of the guardian angels on 2 October. Presumably, Metatron, Uriel and all the others, make their own arrangements.

In more recent times, Pope John XXIII used to send his guardian angel ahead of him whenever he had a difficult meeting to attend, asking that his angel speak with the guardian angels of the other people before he walked in. By this means, he felt the whole tone of the gathering was less hostile and difficult than it may otherwise have been. Perhaps we could send our own guardian angel to the angel of our friend when there has been a misunderstanding between us. Even without a belief in angels, merely intending to ameliorate a future encounter between people would have, it seems, a gentling effect in the long run.

ANGELS IN THE BIBLE

In the Old Testament and in the Acts of the Apostles, angels are sent from Heaven to pass on information, either through visitations, as apparitions, or in dreams. The Bible is *not* the place to look for named angels; only three such angels are to be found (Michael, Raphael and Gabriel) although there are quite a few 'angels of the Lord' moving through the text.

The canonical texts say nothing about the creation of the angels, merely present them as created 'givens', showing them in action. Two apochryphal Jewish texts, the *Book of Jubilees* and the *Book of Enoch*, removed from the Jewish canon long ago by the Pharisees, tell of the creation of the angels. It is in *Enoch* that the story of the lust-filled angels mating with mortal women can be found, and in *Jubilees*, we are told that among the work of God on the first day of creation was the forming of spirits and angels. In this book, it is the angel of the presence who speaks to Moses, explaining creation to him. Here again is the notion that God must have an intermediary, or, as is often the case in Greek mythology, a mere human will be vaporised by God's tremendous appearance. In the New Testament, there are also several 'angels of the Lord' who appear, singly and in crowds, or who quietly bring information in dreams.

Traditionally, it is the angel Gabriel who brings news to the maiden that she is to become the woman at the centre of the Christian teaching of the Incarnation; there are angel choirs singing around the skies on the night of the birth of the baby Jesus. It is an angel in a dream that warns Joseph of the impending 'massacre of the innocents' so that he takes his wife and baby into Egypt. And an angel comforts Jesus in the garden of Gethsemane on the night of his arrest.

Angels have been fairly inactive in history since then. Christian theologians would say that Jesus of Nazareth, as the perfect intermediary, has pre-empted them; that their function has been taken over by one who came to earth from Heaven, visited the dead in Hades, then rejoined his father in Heaven. In Jesus Christ, according to Christian teaching, was—is—a human being capable of penetrating the three worlds; a man who allowed the transformation of the human *to* the Divine *by* the Divine.

To say that there is a lot of scholarly disagreement about angels is a huge understatement. The early Church fathers give conflicting accounts concerning the angelic hierarchy and it is interesting to see where and why early and medieval angelology is in such a muddle. To do this, it's necessary to look at other vital religious beliefs of the common era that have strongly influenced our Judaeo-Christian world—and celestial—view.

Zoroastrianism was the state religion of nearby Iran before and around the early Christian times. It was the religion of King Darius, and Zoroaster or Zarathustra himself (the name means 'rich in camels') was a prophet who sought to influence his people towards monotheism. The Greek historian Herodatus mentions Zoroaster, a Magi, one of the Median tribe, a people of astrologers, magicians and physicians. Just as Lord Buddha, five hundred years earlier, taught his vision of reality as a series interconnected jewelled webs, Zoroaster taught an ethical, loving way of life. He stressed the importance of 'good thoughts'. What does that mean? Does it mean loving, rather than hate-filled thoughts?

One of the definitions of prayer that has occurred to me is this: a thought about someone or something that has as its intention the blessing and healing of the person or situation. More simply put, prayer is loving thought.

Alexander the Great almost wiped out Zoroastrianism and the Muslim conquest of Asia Minor in the seventh century destroyed the remnants, except for a group that migrated to India in the tenth century, the Parsees. However, it was impossible to remove the enormous influence of the Zoroastrian world view. To anyone of Western 'Christian' education, it is extremely familiar. It is a dualistic system, based on two primal spirits, 'the Better and the Bad', between which a person must choose. It is reflected in the popular notion that our 'bad angel' sits on our left shoulder and our 'good angel' on our right. In this tradition, there are holy, immortal beings like angels and there is also the notion that all individuals have guardian spirits. There is a wonderful tradition that reminded me of the very little I understand about particle physics. According to this tradition, each of us has a pre-existing immortal soul which splits when we embody; one part going into the incarnation, the other waiting in its pure state like a sort of innocent doppelgänger until the moment of our death, when it reunites itself with the half that defected into material manifestation. Is our guardian angel then, quite literally our 'better half'?

The Zoroastrians believed that two huge opposing forces, Ahriman, the drive towards the material, and Ahura Mazda, the pure spirit, waged constant conflict. It is these notions that pop up over and over again in the various 'heresies' that have always beset clean-cut orthodox Christianity. They were obviously very deeply ingrained in the early Christian psyche and *not* from Jewish sources. It is important to note that the Hebrew Bible does *not* portray evil powers attacking or threatening the goodness of God or God's creation. This is very much a Zoroastrian notion. It is Ahriman, the spirit who promotes the goodness of the material world, who persuades humans that the physical and the drives and appetites pertaining to the physical are more important than any spiritual life.

Zoroastrian beliefs and practices included charity towards the poor and hospitality towards strangers. There were rituals around sexual and other contact. The Zoroastrian believer tended a sacred fire in his dwelling and after his death, his spirit was believed to haunt the house for three days. (Cremation was regarded with horror; it was considered to be a sin without expiation.) After this, he faced the judgement where his good and bad deeds were weighed in a balance. There were three results: equilibrium, bliss or torture. Certainly pre-Vatican II Catholic readers will notice strong resonances.

However, the Zoroastrian Hell was not eternal. The notion of Hell, with its eternal state of suffering projected infinitely into time, is entirely an invention of the early Christian church. This notion of a vengeful God is true blasphemy. No wonder so many people have turned away from any wish to know of the Divine.

In the second century the Church father Origen records that there were no early doctrines regarding angels, or demons, for that matter. And I'm afraid that it's difficult to look at angels without looking at demons, because the same names tend to pop up in both teams. This is no doubt one of the reasons why the medieval church banned the seemingly popular practice of conjuring angels. It was done in similar manner to the conjuring of demons using the pentacle with the angel's name (the sigil) written in Hebrew around the circle. So conjured, the angel was believed to carry out your will. Prayer and magic have always been confused. In fact, the great Hebrew angel Metatron could be conjured in both diabolical or angelic summonses, depending on the conjurer's intention.

Metatron is a good example of the tangle of angels—as our dualistic Western minds see it. What are we to make of an angel who has a hundred names, one of which is 'the lesser YHWH' or Yahweh (the revealed name of God) who is also one of the angels of the Presence (as Raphael so describes himself: 'I am Raphael, one of the seven angels who stand and enter before the glory of the Lord'), while at the same time is also a great Duke of Hell? Under a couple of his other names, Shemuel or Camael, he is depicted with a leopard's body and is simultaneously ruler of the wicked demons who live on the planet Mars.

Just to make things even more muddled, some say demons are not the same as fallen angels. Tertullian (*c.* 160–220), an influential writer and early father of the Church, worked this out in the third century. According to him, demons came from the sexual intercourse of angels and human women. Another early father of the Church, Justin, teaches that this is where evil comes from. Demons traditionally can breed like us and, like us, they also die; angels are created immortal. Yet Paul mentions evil angels in his vision of the Third Heaven. There, he encountered 'angels of evil, terrible and without pity, carrying savage weapons.' This is in the early days when Hell was still contained within Heaven.

THE ORDERS OF ANGELS

For most early Christian societies God was seen as the centre of all creation, of all things spiritual and physical. The exceptions were the Gnostic Christians, who could not make sense of an eternal, timeless, matter-free God creating things that were totally unlike their Creator—material beings doomed to time and space. The Gnostics could not find God in the physical world at all. They saw human consciousness *imprisoned* in the material body, deluded by the illusions of matter.

According to the orthodox system everything radiated out from this centre—this God—and the further away anything was from the godly epicentre, the more dense, the less 'pure' it became. Traditionally there were nine 'rings' to this core, a bit like a huge, celestial all-day sucker, with the 'taint' of matter first occurring like an ominous shadow at the third ring—the territory of the angelic order known as 'Thrones'. 'At the third stroke it will be the beginning of matter, time and space!'

Angels are arranged in levels of three; and within each of these levels are three further orders or ranks. Revolving around the Presence, forming the first ring around the innermost core of Godness, are the highest, the most magnificent of angelic choirs, the seraphs or seraphim. The seraphs chant the endless praise that Catholics at Mass briefly and automatically join in with at the *Sanctus*: 'Holy, holy, holy ... Holy is the Lord of Hosts, the whole earth is full of his glory ...' a quotation from a great Hebrew prayer. But because—according to Jewish theologians—angels speak Hebrew, what they actually say is '*Kadosh, kadosh, kadosh ...*'

The word 'seraph' seems to come from two Hebrew roots: *rapha* meaning 'healer' seen most obviously in the name of the great archangel, Raphael, who is traditionally associated with healing and whose name translates as 'the healing of God' and *ser* meaning 'higher being' or 'guardian angel'. This *ser* is the same root we meet in '*ser*pent' and is one of the reasons why the serpent has been traditionally associated with wisdom and healing; the serpent was sacred in the groves of Aesculapius, the great healer of the ancients. Moses set up a bronze serpent on a pole in the desert, to heal the

Israelites when they were afflicted by the bites of poisonous snakes.

The serpent and the tree feature in other mythologies. The Assyrians had a Tree of Everlasting Life. The Chaldeans had a tradition of lightning snakes that pierced the earth and made it fertile and it is thought that seraphim had their origins in the snake of the ancient Chaldeans. It's interesting to note that those snaky lightning flashes during storms *do*, in fact, improve soil fertility, by increasing the level of available nitrogen in the atmosphere. And it certainly adds depth to the Eden story to go on a little etymological journey with and around the serpent. Even the Genesis writer, harking back to earlier traditions of earth wisdom and the snake, notes that the serpent is the most 'subtle' of the created beings.

Only last century, Cardinal Newman, in his belief that all spiritual being is intellectual, wrote this of the 'building' of Heaven:

The smallest portions of this edifice,
cornice or freize, or balustrade or stair,
the very pavement is made up of life —
of holy, blessed and immortal beings
who hymn their Maker's praise continually.

PART TWO

Grace of Angels

WHY DO WE NEED ANGELS?

Too many teachers condemn; or at best, exhort. We have been condemned and exhorted since preaching started. Look around you at the world we live in. It hasn't worked anywhere.

Apart from the extremely rigid ones, religious preachers rarely tell me anything I don't already 'approve' of as a 'good idea'. But they never tell me how they practise this 'good idea' every day. They never come down from their superior place and show me how they do it. A person is not taught how to fly an aircraft by the instructor telling her over and over that this is how it should be done. This is why the flying instructor gets into the cabin with the student and stays close beside her, lesson after lesson. This is how humans learn anything—in relationship with another, being shown, not told. Unfortunately, few of us learn how to be fully human when we're growing up because we are told how to be, but not shown how to do it, by people who were themselves only told and never shown. There is a whole world of experts full of theory about how humans should be.

People look to experts to tell them how to be instead of examining their own hearts. Look at the world we live in. Sadly my teachers never showed me what I needed to understand because they were never honest.

In childhood, we are taught that it is bad to tell a lie. And we are taught this by liars. We are taught that it is wrong to hit people who are smaller than we are by people who only hit people smaller than they are. We are taught that it is very naughty to use violence to get our way by people who do exactly that. What a mess this creates, generation after generation.

We need angels badly. Not up in Heaven, not on our walls in frames, but down here right next to us ready to link our hands with the hands of the people around us. If angels are nothing more than a device, a conceit describing loving thoughts, we need that energy, that love, that ability to connect us with each other as we move to open our narrow, separated minds into the vastness of the Kingdom of Heaven—the interconnected jewelled webs. However, a person likes to see reality.

PRAYER TO THE ANGEL OF CONNECTEDNESS (1)

Angel of jewelled webs between all things,
seeker of the lost and lonely,
weaving them all into the sacred fabric
of our Oneness.
Please hear me when I call to you.
Remind me all is One and One is All.
That I am part of everybody else
and they of me. That there is no
'out there' or 'not like me'.
No 'them', just 'us'.
No 'bad' or 'good' but only lost or loving.
When I forget this truth and point my finger
accusing part of us of hurting me,
gather us all in to your heart.
Hug us tight with reassuring love.
Remind us of our total innocence.

ANGELS OF RELATIONSHIPS

Real relationship is established by sharing our selves, our sameness; the ordinary similarities of our lives. It is the sharing of these ordinary things, our loving, our fearing, our hating, our suffering, our yearning, that creates trust, and trust is where relationship grows.

As I got older and looked around with eyes that could see, I started to understand that in a world where true relationship is almost always destroyed, by virtue of this moralising superiority, a power structure would have to develop to enforce the teachings. The desire for relationship brings us together; not indoctrination, not coercion through fear of punishment. Fear can only isolate and alienate.

The first relationship with a spiritual companion is usually the guardian angel, for children of Catholic background. Jewish children since Rabbinic times have recited this bedtime prayer:

In the name of the Lord, God of Israel!
May Michael be at my right hand and Gabriel at my left,
before me Uriel, and behind me Raphael
and above my head, the Divine Presence of God.

The Divine presence of God is called in Jewish terms 'the Shekinah'—the holy spirit of God. What a prayer!

This prayer sounds more powerful and commanding than the 'Angel of God' recitation of my childhood:

Angel of God, my guardian dear
to whom God's love commits me here
ever this day be at my side
to light and guard, to rule and guide. Amen.

Refusing to grow, staying with the known is to stagnate. Life has a way of pushing and pulling us when we try to dig in against growth. It is a fact demonstrated every day by those who die of an addiction that many people prefer to die rather than change. Life is flexible; death is rigid.

Relationship is flexible; power is rigid. In relationship, if I am different and this is difficult for you, you make room for this and we talk it over. We negotiate because we have equal rights. In a power system, where we do not have equal rights, and there is only one way of doing things, if I am seen as being different, I am sacked. Excommunicated.

The fluidness of an angel, whether it is understood as thought in a mind or some sort of physical charge of power, is full of movement, of flexibility. An angel is life surging.

PRAYER TO THE ANGEL OF CONNECTEDNESS (2)

Angel, I am out of kilter with my friend,
out of relationship.
Maybe we have quarrelled. Or maybe just the icy waste of distance
Invoked by my disdain for conflict, separates our hearts.
Remind me once again that conflict is not bad.
Teach me that conflict,
respectfully expressed, is the place where spaciousness appears
and new ground grows.
Conflict, respectfully expressed, is the garden of God.
New land reclaimed from the Department of Defence.
A place to make a garden.
Teach me how to listen to my friend whom I have hurt.
And teach her how to hear me when I tell her of my pain.
Hold us both in that tremendous place where, honest with each
other, we are humble and attentive.

Show me how to transform this anxiety.
Hold us as we listen to each other and embrace.

Relationship is another way of saying 'compassion'. Compassion stands at heart level and doesn't see 'important people' or 'insignificant people'. Compassion only sees 'us'. Compassion is not pity, which looks down at 'poor them'. Nor is it sympathy which leans over from an untouched place to comfort another's suffering. Compassion recognises the touching truth of our human nature; that we are all born to suffer and to die, no matter what physical differences in status might be perceived, and in the time given to us, either spin out into mindlessness, chasing ambition, security, sex, power, real estate, the headlock of intellectualising, religiosity, television, creativity, addictions of any sort, or face the truth of these facts and find a way of living that makes them bearable.

Relationship supports the person that you are, while practising honesty within that framework. When there is conflict in a friendship, it is always a conflict between peers. Sometimes I have to walk away from relationships because I simply don't have the wisdom or the expertise to stay balanced. When I do this, I remember that it is not because the other person is 'bad' or 'wrong', but because I am not mature enough nor deep enough yet not to lose my ground.

PRAYER TO THE ANGEL OF DISTANCE

(For Cecile and all of us)

My friend and I are separate, Angel,
apart and distanced by our own unskilfulness.
My terrors and my fears surround me, crowd me,
whispering the *no goods, hopeless, nevers,* that I fear.
And in the misty gulf between us, the monsters take their shapes:
Abandonment and howling Desolation:
the Accuser shrieks for vengeance on my friend.
And I am half convinced this should be done.
Angel, fill the space with golden light.

Change this gulf into a temple.
Turn the monsters into daisies and their shrieking into grace.
Let me play and sing unhindered under trees that love has made.
Let me greet my friend with flowers as we meet beneath their shade.

ANGELS, MIND AND FOCUS

The wisdom of ordinariness can be developed by examining how your own mind is set up and this can be the beginning of self understanding. Our minds are full of mess, our own and other people's, and often it is very difficult for us to focus clearly on something that we need to do. The mighty angel Raphael is the great healer and it might be a good idea to ask for his assistance with focus because help will be needed to start on the mess of mind.

One of the facts about mind is this: we develop whatever we focus on. If you think of your daily world as the field, focus is the light that shines on certain parts of your field. Focus switches around as we value or devalue what we perceive.

A mind can contain a rag bag of old, distorted memories, bits and pieces of other people's injunctions and prohibitions, old rules set up by perhaps long dead parents and teachers, bits of junk from old books, images from films and pictures, vague fears and desires—and this is just part of the landscape.

It can be a lifetime's work to start letting go of this stuff; letting the habitual old system fall away. Some people end up destroying their own minds completely. Many people are addicted to the contents of their mind, their manner of thinking, and don't want to let go, even when the contents of their mind create great discomfort for them and the people around them in daily living.

Years ago, I started to realise that just because a belief was in my mind that *didn't make it either true or valuable*. After a few years, this realisation meant that I was no longer so attached to the furniture of my mind, my thoughts, my feelings, my ideas, my beliefs. Sure, they were mine, and that was nice, and they helped make me *me* and not someone else, but apart from that, so what? Like Tinkerbell, I suppose the attachment to them shrank and faded in importance.

PRAYER TO THE ANGEL OF THE INNER TEMPLE

Between the spaces of my breath
there is an opening.
Between the boiling clouds of mindless thinking
teeming thoughts and dead ideas,
shoulds and ego goals and ought to's,
there is a stillness
where shines a steady brilliant light.
Angel, guide me to the temple
of the Is Now Ever Shall Be.
There I'll rest a while in peace.

One of the most important aspects of the notion of an angel is the angel's ability to move between worlds that, in the normal course of events, have no bridge between them. Perhaps this is one reason for them being depicted with wings. It is a hopeful and beautiful symbol; that disparate worlds can be reconnected by an angel. Theologians tell us that angels are in a constant state of perfection, and from this state simply express the truth of their being with perfection. We humans are not so endowed. We are tied to the physical; locked, it seems, in bodies of meat and bones. Some would say that's all we are—just clever animals who enjoy art galleries and good wines and sharing clever ideas. And in our upside down world, the fear around the notions of 'growth' may seem to be well founded.

Too often, the other end of youth means sickness and frailty and becoming attached to medical conditions and illnesses—shutdown rather than growth. In this world, growth is inextricably tied to ageing and decline; I sense a despairing, unvoiced 'what's the point?' in many people. Why grow and develop—why do anything at all, when at the other end, later if not sooner, death waits with bony hands to take it all away? It's a good question and one that may never be answered glibly; what is the point of a person's life?

I think it has something to do with knowing oneself. Knowing what I am leads me towards knowing what I am for; what my purpose is. This sort of knowing is not found on the surface of life.

PRAYER TO ASRAEL, ANGEL OF DEATH

The ones who fear you most have never lived.
They fear the shadow of your stormy wings,
closed off, resistant to the call to love.
Usurping the Divine with their harsh judgement,
living lives already stiff and cold.
Awaken us to see that now is all there is;
that life and love can only happen *now*.
Not later, not one day, not when I have more time . . .
But right this minute opening up to love
and letting go of our cruel thoughts
where love is judged away.
The ones who fear you most have never lived.

Open our hearts to Now and all Now's richness
so that they will be opened up to you.
Teach me, dark Asrael, the way to live.
In learning that, I learn the way to die.

If everything that is not of our essence is removed, the question 'What am I for?' can no longer be answered with the superficial answers that once satisfied, such as 'I am a pilot and I exist to fly aircraft'. Or 'I am a writer and I exist to write books'. Or 'I am a mother and I exist to nurture my children'. No. These answers will not do in the last analysis. Because one day the pilot will be grounded, the writer will put down the pen, the children will grow up and go away. There comes a day when we are left only with self; a subject without any more predicates, and the question 'What am I for?' becomes acute in its demand to be answered.

Once a person has swung round from the false (but usually tenaciously held) 'I am different from everybody else in the world' to the mundane, boring truth of 'I am the same as everybody else in the world', the sense of being separate can start to slip away and a person can become ordinary. I think this is the beginning of humility.

PRAYER TO THE ANGEL OF ORDINARINESS (Inspired by Penne)

Angel, I'm forgetting again and trying instead to be something
I'm not:
'forgiving' when I can't be,
'loving' when I'm not . . .
Help me stop trying and let me remember myself.
My own ordinary self.
As ordinary as this hand that I reach out to other ordinary hands.
As ordinary as this self that I've lived with many years.
As ordinary as all the other selves around me.
All of us fearing death, suffering and the absence of love.
All of us wanting the same ordinary things; love, joy and freedom
from pain.
Angel, gather your wings around us.
Love, joy and freedom from pain.

Whisper to me how holy this ordinariness is.
What else is there to want?

How are we to live with the knowledge of those waiting, bony hands? How can we make a life that is spacious and peaceful and comfortable to live in and one that is not about grasping and controlling, trying to hold on to the tiny pleasures that we believe this world presents to us, before we sicken and die?

I have come to think that every human heart contains the answer to this and other ultimate questions. But I also think these answers are locked away until something opens those hearts to the truth that they contain. Perhaps it is an angel that starts the thaw of a glacial human heart? Perhaps there is an angel of soft tears?

PRAYER TO THE ANGEL OF SOFT TEARS

Melt me, Angel. Melt this hard and clever mind I use instead of heart.
Soften and stroke away this hard 'I know'
this harsh 'You fool'.
Let me be the child again. Bend down to me and whisper of the little one who doesn't know and doesn't blame
but only puts her hand up into her mother's and trots along all trusting.
To the circus or the gas-chamber the little ones go.
And we, too, must go. At the appointed time let go the breath, let go the body. All of us must die.
Melt me with this knowing. All of us are dying.
Let us take each other's hands, Angel, and sing along the way.

In these closing years of one of the most horrendous centuries on earth, isn't it eccentric to be thinking of angels? to consider writing a book about them in any way but amused superiority or New Age breathlessness? 'Channel your very own Angel!' Angels, indeed.

And yet as we lose touch with our deep truth, and spiral away further from ourselves and our centre in the agonising busy-ness of chasing careers, building additions to homes, pushing children to get higher marks, fighting our partners and in-laws, beating ourselves up at the gym, getting ulcers and other diseases, undermining our colleagues so as to get that promotion, perhaps an angel—even the notion of an angel—could build a temporary bridge, the beginning of the scaffolding necessary for the job of sacred restoration?

PRAYER TO THE ANGEL OF ACCEPTANCE

If I am here, then I am meant to be
and part of this whole world that I can see.
Joined with all of us and they with me.
How often I forget this, feeling cut off and alone.
Feeling I'm a lost soul, a million miles from home.
Take my hand, accepting Angel, join it up with other hands.
So that we can walk together,
live and love and truly know
we are all part of each other, part of everything and all.

ANGELS AND PRAYER

To pray is the opposite of 'to know.' This is because prayers come out of the deepest sense of human 'not knowing'; when a person comes into a situation or event in life and simply does not know what to do and realises this, the only words left are most often prayers.

This place takes a long time to find. Some people never find it in a lifetime and they are drawn to keep trying, pushing, pulling, working harder, finding more ways of manipulating, determined to find a solution. When we do this we become desperate to impose our will onto an obdurate circumstance or person. Thinking, thinking, thinking, never coming to understand that thoughts just lead to more thoughts, never coming to see that mind is locked in on itself, endlessly circling in compulsive thinking.

But sometimes some of these people, usually after many years of trying to enforce solutions, many years of suffering because this way of living is immensely exhausting and painful, find that they have reached this place where they admit that they simply don't know what to do. They have come up against the wall of their own ego's limitations. In some cases, deep depression results. Suicide is not uncommon.

If we can stay in this place of deep anxiety and not rush off into 'new' thoughts, yet another 'solution', there is the chance for an immense shift in mind to take place.

This humble place is sacred ground; a place empty now of the thoughts churned out by the sausage machine of thinking; a sacred space in which a prayer can be born. It can be as simple as 'I just don't know any more', or even more simple, 'help me'.

This holy ground leads the prayer-maker at first into deeper and deeper levels of not knowing; of not knowing what she is doing, or why she is doing it, of feeling stupid, of wondering what her friends might think if they knew, of not really knowing what to ask for, not knowing to whom the prayer is addressed, not knowing if there is someone there who can hear, and certainly not knowing if the prayer will be answered. In this way, prayer leads the prayer-maker even further into terra incognita; further away from the safety and staleness of the known and habitual thought systems.

To ask for help is the bravest thing we can do in a world where the greatest disgust is reserved for those who can't 'hold it together', those who 'break down', those who say they can't do it any more. Even those who weep are often viewed with unease, told with embarrassment to 'pull themselves together' by others who themselves long ago lost the gift of tears.

PRAYER TO THE ANGEL OF HEALING

Raphael, cover me with your healing wings.
Let radiance flow from Heaven to my heart.
Let my dis-ease be lessened,
my pain softened. Heal in me any hard,
unloving thoughts.
Softly ease all judgement from my mind.

Leave in their place acceptance of the way things are.
Teach me that acceptance is not defeat but choice,
and from surrender health and peace can grow.
I place in your hands all my fears and worries and ask that
into my opened heart you pour the balm of peace.

Pharmaceutical companies make thousands of millions of dollars creating and marketing drugs that sedate and block out deep feelings so that people can 'pull themselves together', not cry and keep going. We're horrified to hear of sportspeople who injure themselves badly, inject an opiate and run back onto the field for the second half, numbed to the pain. We wonder what further damage they must be doing to the already injured tissue.

But, few people wonder what it means that people in spiritual pain take drugs to avoid their lives. What further damage might that cause? Wouldn't it be wiser for us to see that in many cases our suffering comes from living with an immense sadness and hurt? That our suffering is real and has a real cause? Then we can take appropriate action towards changing these painful conditions instead of numbing the agony of perhaps decades of unresolved, unvoiced conflict, generations of deep and ancient unhealed wounds, handed down in families, that have created isolated, alienated people, cut off from our unique sense of self.

There is certainly growing evidence that many forms of disease occur as a result of depressed immune systems, and that the relieving of resentments and old hatreds, empowers the immune system so that natural healing can occur. There are medical people like the American surgeon and author, Bernie Siegal, who have no doubt that the resolving and forgiving of resentments and hatreds, even in the terminally ill, can bring about the healing of many forms of deadly disease.

PRAYER TO THE ANGEL OF JOINING

Holy Angel of all of us, Angel of Joining.
Take my hand and show me how it all belongs to me.
We are all here for each other. No-one is alone.
My bony little cranium wants to practise 'lock-out'.
My thin and frightened soul believes it is alone.
Open my heart and show me the enormity of truth.
Open my heart to the flash flood of Love
that sweeps away all barriers, all fortresses of fear.
Show me Heaven filled with joined and joyful people,
singing, loving, laughing in the radiance of Life.

PRAYER AND NEGATIVE MIND

There are too many people living joyless lives full of suspicion, resentment or hostility towards everyone else. If we are attached to negative thoughts, or negative mind, we will eventually bring about the destruction of our true mind as it moves deeper and deeper towards hatred. It is a matter of pure self-interest for us to decide against supporting negativity when it comes up in mind, as it will. It's not a matter of pretending that dreadful things don't happen in this world; they do. But whether or not we attach to this information in a mental embrace as it were, and hold onto it, and allow it to hold onto us, is a choice we are always making.

Make no mistake about it, to most people, negative mind feels good. Those crowds of people gathered outside courthouses, screaming, aren't there for the sake of justice, truth or clarity. They're there venting their hatred because it feels good. Nor is it really a matter of trying to be 'nice' or 'good' or 'holy' to start letting go of attachment to negative mind—judgement, resentment and hatred. It's a question of deciding whether you wish to destroy your own mind or not.

When negativity comes up, as inevitably it will, this is the perfect time for prayer. Give the negative thought to an angel to carry away and defuse for you because the teachers of wisdom say that negative mind gradually loses its power if we don't attach to it. Minds can be healed.

PRAYER TO THE ANGEL WHO DEFENDS AGAINST NEGATIVE MIND

Protect me, Angel from this dark attraction,
the glamorous glitter of negative mind.
Read all about it! cry the papers.
Listen to this! screams the DJ.
This busy nastiness, this cruel wanting to know,
drawing me towards other people's suffering;
curiosity without love.
They call it 'keeping up to date' with every vile encounter,
every shocking act of hatred, every nasty bit of business.
They scream it from the airwaves on the hour, the half-hour
and somewhere in my mind the snake of dark attraction
lifts his head
and wants to know it all, swell up on it, and fill my mind.
Protect me, Angel, from his glittering scales.

It could also be valuable to keep in mind what writer Jean Bedford's mother used to say: 'We all have the right to go to Hell in our own buckets.' And time and time again, when the bucket finally arrives in Hell, the person in the bucket has at last come to the place where she can be clear and whole-minded, possibly for the first time in her life, about never wanting to be in Hell again and point her bucket in the direction of Heaven. She may have arrived at the place of prayer, and know it for the first time.

This is what the angel of acceptance might whisper to me:

Acceptance lets people be.

Acceptance doesn't have to do anything.

Acceptance doesn't have to agree or disagree.

Acceptance is quiet and peaceful and all 'againstness' can softly dissolve in it. It has no moving parts to create friction.

Acceptance gently acknowledges the truth of how things are.

Acceptance comes with a gentle sigh of relief.

Ah. So that's how it is.

ANGELS, PRAYING AND THE UNKNOWN

If you've never prayed before, be prepared for huge changes to start almost immediately. You will need an angel with you. I know a woman who prayed to nothing in particular while she was on a train heading north. She remembered that a friend had once told her 'When your back's against the wall, pray to the universe for help.' Her back was against a wall. She was an atheist addict with no money, no job, no friends, because naturally all she could do with people was use them, and she was going north to suicide after she used her last dope. So her prayer was, 'if there's anyone there, help me.'

Within three days of this prayer, and without even now understanding how this came about, she was back in Sydney in a detox unit. It's six and half years since she last used drugs and she now has a satisfying, creative job, good friends who love her and whom she now can love, and her life gets better and better.

She is still completely agnostic. All she knows is that something happened. This is just one of hundreds of such cases I know about prayer suddenly swinging a person's life around. Nor is belief required. Belief, as much as disbelief, is only an idea in a mind; pictures hanging on mind's wall. It is not a belief that makes the difference but a movement in mind. Prayer is movement towards the unknown; the leap into the abyss. The angels rush to your side to hold you up.

PRAYER TO THE ANGEL OF THE UNKNOWN REGION

Angel, all my life I've feared to look inside,
feared what I might find.
And so I wouldn't look at me,
preferring always to put the blame 'out there'.
If they weren't so awful, I would be quite sweet.
If he'd just be different, I'd be quite content.

I battled on, confused as to why this *always*
happened with this person,
why I always lost it under those circumstances.
That's just me, I told myself.
I'm like that.
But you know the truth and the truth is
I don't know what I'm like.
Because I don't know why I do half the things I do,
and the other half I didn't want to do until too late.
I'm prepared now to examine my behaviour.
Just calmly, clearly help me look at me.
Teach me this is not about blame, not about 'bad' or 'good',
But the decision to fear or love.
I'm starting to understand that how I am has consequences.
I'm starting to see that what I do creates effects.
Did I think I was invisible to others simply because
I was invisible to me?
I admit I have no knowledge of myself. Angel, help me see.
Til I can see the picture, it's not possible to change.

ANGELS, PRAYER AND GOODNESS

There is a deep satisfaction that comes with living your own goodness. It is not at all the same thing as being 'happy' although great happiness can be experienced. Sometimes, living truthfully can bring great pain. But, once it has been experienced, this deep satisfaction is so essential to one's ability to breathe and to be, that it becomes a necessary condition for one's continued existence. This satisfaction seems to come from relaxing into the truth of one's own goodness and living according to the light of that goodness. It sounds simple and it is. But it means lots of unlearning and letting go of non-essentials, and that takes time and clarity to start discovering what those are.

Goodness deep within a person is a warm radiance that makes us want to draw closer to that person. Unlike cleverness, which dazzles with its brilliance and complexity as it builds and branches, goodness has no moving parts; it is a steady state. It is simplicity. To be with a good person is to experience steadiness and balance. Clever people, and those who desire to emulate cleverness, often find this dull because they have become so accustomed—addicted perhaps—to constant stimulation that they experience simplicity as stupid. Goodness has nothing to do with pious mental structures in a mind, but can be recognised as a way of being and living. It is fuelled by a generous spirit. Good people can't help giving. And they don't even notice that they're doing it.

PRAYER TO THE ANGEL OF GOODNESS

In me, good Angel, is the flame in every human heart.
Perhaps it burns low and is forgotten as I run
around trying to be good.
perhaps I've walled my heart off, fearful of its famishment
Remind me, Angel, that I am good

because I am just ordinary and because it is my nature
and goodness is part of the ordinary nature of a person.
Remind me that I can love
because I am the same as anyone else.
I believed love was some rare gem
and only great saints had it.
I was mistaken. The great saints know at depth
what I am coming to see;
that love is not in saintly acts but in me.
Help me stay and listen to the truth.
Help my sad heart open to its love.
This ordinary me.

PRAYER AND RESPECT

Leave people alone and let them do things the way they choose to. This is simple respect. And as you withdraw your desire to dominate and control, to have everyone be like you, think like you and do like you do, you leave a place of respect, a place where the other person can truly be himself, a place where other things can start to grow for both of you. Angel space.

I know from experience that if some of these simple acts of respect are applied to daily living, relationships that had seemed beyond help can become healed. Angels move into such places and fill them with love.

PRAYER TO THE ANGEL OF RESPECT

Remind me, Angel, I have no right
to force my will onto my friend.
Give me space and softness around this strong desire of mine.
Prise it from this grasping mind
and let it float with all the other wantings I have had.
Look. Look at them all!
Let me see that getting them has never brought me peace.
Here I am, still wanting something else again.
Nor will this one, even if I get my way, satisfy for long
Too soon comes the next one crowding, nagging.
Space and softness let the laughter in.
'Here I go again, wanting, wanting.
Funny person, always wanting.'
Let me laugh at me,
otherwise the wanting may become a weapon
pointed at my friend.

Sometimes I can't sleep and it's because of a headache, a clogged nose, restless mind, grief or some other preoccupation. There is a simple and effective prayer path through this. It doesn't need any belief system or any spiritual skills. Simply bring to mind all the people in the world who may be experiencing discomfort in this moment, whether they are restless and in pain alone at home, in hospitals, in flats, under bridges—wherever they are. Something moves. Something happens when mind reaches out to join with itself and the next thing I know whenever I do this, is it's morning. This has never failed me and it's prayer at its most effective and practical and without any piousness getting in the way.

ANGELS, PRAYER AND TEACHING

The prayer system I was taught as a child was always about ego wishes. There was no notion at all of surrender, of letting all things be the way they are without imposing our wills onto them. It was presumed that the Divine was already in complete agreement regarding a pass in an exam, the healing of a sick relative, a fine day for the sports carnival and our school to win the final. We told God what was needed. But whatever the Divine is, it is not to be domesticated, nor harnessed in any way to our ends. To only pray like this is to try and squash the universe into an egg cup.

Children learn by listening, by watching, examining, feeling; not by preached words. Children have a sense of the whole person who is saying something to them, and if this person's manner belies her words, the child will feel uneasy. According to the communication experts, words form only a small part of expression. Research shows that in any presentation before a group of people, 55 per cent of the impact is determined by body language—posture, gesture and eye contact—38 per cent by the tone of voice and only 7 per cent by the content! (*Introducing NLP*, Joseph O'Connor and John Seymour, p17)

'Show don't tell' is the rule for good writing. It is also the rule for good teaching. A learner needs to be shown, not told. Many people have been so badly burned by the cruel teachings of ignorant teachers, that it is not possible for them to look at the word 'prayer' without flinching. Anything to do with God, church or religion for instance, causes instant revulsion. It's a sad fact that many 'religious' people adhere to their rigid 'rightness' and disapprove of others who have different ways of being in the world.

Because, throughout history, many teachings were not presented as great mysteries to be pondered but were enforced as facts to be 'believed in' (under pain of eternal torture), dogmata were the result. These 'spiritual facts' (surely a contradiction in terms) were often taught by rigid people, who had little self-love or self-awareness.

PRAYER TO THE ANGEL OF THE TRUTH

The Truth is free and clear and simple.
Never hidden, closed in secret writings
that only special, clever people know.
Those who try to hide you, Angel,
always fail. Your radiance is too brilliant to be
contained in crypts
and those who try to imprison you find you've
slipped through their bars like sunshine.
The truth is always simple.
I am here and I am loved and that is all I need to know.
And when I really know it, even truth itself can grow.

Without any understanding of what a belief structure is, of how it is set up in mind, of how ego attaches to the structure and calls that particular idea 'the truth', these teachers produced many people who simply duplicated this unexamined system. To be different was to be wrong, to be wrong was to be bad. There was no acceptance for individual differences. Anyone who disagreed with their particular belief structures, was not only wrong, but was rebelling against God. It's not hard to see where guilt might start growing. These teachers presumed to know the mind of God and be speaking on God's behalf. God wouldn't let you enrol in Heaven if you did not adhere to the dogmata to pass the exam; there was no respecting of individual differences. One of the beautiful things that is constant about angel visitations in the Bible, is the deep respect the angelic visitor accords the person to whom he is appearing.

The teachers of the system that trained me and who believed that the intellect held all the answers, and who seemed to take seriously the notion of 'human reason' despite all the evidence to the contrary, had this to say of mysticism: 'It begins in a mist, ends in a schism and has a big "I" in the middle.' They condemned what they could not comprehend.

Despite this, some rare and wonderful souls, century after century, have always found a secret door in the wall, and moved from the heresies they were taught towards a spiritual life that developed and matured as they grew. There are very few of them. They are stamped with joy, the hallmark of the teacher of Truth, and it is beautiful to be in their company in the books that many of them wrote. The only way to teach love is by loving.

The revolutionary insight of Buddhism, says Sogyul Rinpoche, teacher-writer of Tibetan wisdom for Western readers, is that life and death are in the mind and nowhere else. Mind is revealed as the universal basis of experience—the creator of happiness and the creator of suffering. There are many aspects of mind, but the part that needs looking at is ordinary mind or 'daily mind', what the Buddhists call *sem*—the place where wanting, validating, arguing, thinking, creating, manipulating and judging go on. This part of mind flares up in anger, indulges in negative and hateful judgements about other people or self, aspires to what it calls 'love' which is always very partial and self-centred because it is based in my personal 'approval' of someone. This part of mind, *sem* mind, is likened to a candle flame in an open doorway. It is always on the go. This part of mind is where we habitually operate from—the so-called 'rational mind'.

Except for the rare glimpses of the true nature of mind (perhaps in meditation or perhaps as just a gift), of 'pure, pristine awareness, that is both cognisant, intelligent and radiant', most of us only have experience of this ordinary *sem* mind. This is the part of mind where human hatred starts to grow. In *sem* mind is the potential for both domestic violence and world war. Any spiritual development entails the practice of letting go of this part of mind; coming to see its partiality, its tininess, its total selfishness and subjectivity, and its essential meaninglessness. Enlightenment is coming into the state, says Sogyul Rinpoche, of 'your flawless, present awareness, cognisant and empty, naked and awake'.

PRAYER TO THE ANGEL OF LIGHT

Way beyond the place of knowing,
past the place called 'Understand',
is the sacred site I've yearned for,
holy space my heart demands.

Angel, you know every thought
that brain puts in the way of Mind.
Clear the sky of all my dark clouds
so the light of Truth can shine.
Take my hand and lead me there
to the place where Radiance flows,
in the peace where stillness dances.
Take me to our long-held Home.

ANGELS, PRAYER AND LOVE

As we move through our lives and deal with the immediate suffering and problems life presents each of us, the desire to experience truth starts to take precedence over other goals. Eventually, this is what prayer does. It gently moves us in any of the millions of ways home, however home may present itself to each of us. Love doesn't care what it's called. 'The glory of God', said Father Iraneus a long, long time ago, 'is a human being fully alive'. To become the glory of God calls for all the courage a person can muster and the humility to ask for the help of another in whatever form this may take. And through this humility, a person can develop the capacity for love, and through this capacity will flow the desire to know and to serve Other, whether this is understood in terms of the Divine or more simply other human spirits.

Some people call this Other, this hugeness of life, this place where mind meets everyone and everything, this attitude of compassion for everyone and everything God or Jesus or Buddha or Allah. In New Age terms, it is sometimes Universal intelligence, Universal Mind. This mind, the wise say, is never accusatory or judgemental. It never interferes in our way of being. It simply loves. If the first law of real estate is position, position, position, the first law of the spirit is freedom, freedom, freedom. Freedom to be who we are, freedom to do whatever is necessary to find the truth for ourselves. Freedom to make as many 'mistakes' (in whose judgement are these mistakes, anyway?) as it takes. Freedom to live as deeply and fully as possible. Freedom not to toe the line.

Freedom not to stay safe. Freedom to take the huge risk of loving without condition.

PRAYER TO THE ANGEL OF FREEDOM

Holy Angel, free me from the Egypt of my mind.
Making bricks for small, dark huts; stale habitual thinking.
Driven by my masters—security and gold—
I live a life of slavery.
Angel, take hold of me and lead me to the desert.
In the desert there is freedom from the tyranny of old
ways of thinking, being, living,
In the desert there is terror as I move
away from Known, this idol I have lived by
in the land of death and gold.
In the desert there are beasts that howl at night
'*Slave, go back*!'

Angel I'm afraid.
In the desert will I find the water that I need?
In the desert is there food?
An oasis for refreshment, trees and shade and breeze?
I'll never know unless I go and if I stay
I'll perish as a slave.
Angel, stay beside me. Be with me as I go.

With prayer, I can have the courage to see that the anger and the greed and hatred and jealousy that exist in the world also exist in me. And it is my responsibility to deal with that part of it that's in me. I don't even have to be a theist to see that my wishes and desires will always be partisan and based on personality and therefore 'selfish' by definition. I cannot see a bigger picture unless I release my clutching hold on my desires and wants. Through prayer, I can surrender to a higher wisdom, even if it is only the wisdom of the nature of things. I remember a time when the cynic in me said, 'This is all illusion. Everything is created in my mind.' And another part of me offered: 'Very well, it may be so. But if it is all illusion, why not live by an illusion that sustains and supports you rather than one that tears down and destroys all reason for living? Can't make any difference in reality if it's all illusion, Gabrielle.'

In the long run, if everything is illusion, it doesn't matter. But in the short run, while we live these possible illusions, there is a choice between a peaceful mind in a person living a peaceful life, or a person living a life of calamitous inner and outer suffering. If I bring my muddles to whatever this wider wisdom might be, even if it is nothing more than surrendering to the way things are rather than clutching onto my habitual ways of 'solving' them, where I'm doomed to apply nothing more than what I already know, and apply it harder, perhaps it is possible that I am allowing a space for change to begin within. It is commonplace that insanity consists of doing the same thing over and over again, each time expecting a different outcome. If I can be taught to release my grasp, to allow things to be the way they are, and find other ways of dealing with my fear, hatred and anger rather than projecting them onto other people and situations, perhaps real peace can eventually grow within this person. This is the beginning of spiritual responsibility. Nothing can change until I take this step.

PRAYER TO THE ANGEL OF PEACE

I seek the peace that passes understanding
And past my understanding is this world of change.
Nor is it possible to grasp the mind of God.
I seek the peace that passes understanding.
Release me, Angel, from the fight to understand.
Hold me, Angel, in your warm wings
while I disengage from Mind
and find in Heart
the peace I vainly sought in many things.

PRAYER AND INNER HEALTH

There was an 'experiment in prayer' carried out by the cardiologist, Dr. Randolph Byrd, formerly a professor at the University of California. A computer randomly assigned the names of 393 recovering cardiac patients to either a group of people who prayed for them, or a group of people who didn't pray for them. This was a classic double-blind experiment, with neither the patients nor the medical staff knowing which group any of the coronary patients were in. The results were astonishing. Not only did fewer of the 'prayed for' people die, but as a group, those patients had five times less need for antibiotics, were three times less likely to develop pulmonary oedema and did not require breathing tubes. If this had been a drug test, the pharmaceutical company would have been jubilant.

Prayer works because it is an acknowledgment of relationship, an acknowledgment of the truth of how things are. Prayer is one of Buddha's jewelled webs connecting reality together. By holding your name in my mind in a loving way, I am saying 'You are a beloved part of everything that is'. I am acknowledging the connected nature of all things. Whether you know this or not, or believe this or not, is irrelevant. The truth is not dependent on anyone's belief to make it true. The truth simply is because it is true. That's why it doesn't matter whether you believe in God or not. If God is, your belief or lack of it doesn't affect this fact; if God is not, your belief or lack of it makes no difference either.

Prayer is about living at the deepest level of ourselves. It cannot be taught or explained, only experienced. It is not about reciting rote formulae, in an attempt to procure a desired outcome.

PRAYER TO THE ANGEL OF TRUE PRAYER

Gently show me, praying Angel,
how to pray with my true soul.
Help me not to clutch at outcomes,
not misuse prayer to gain control.
Help me see that praying truly
moves towards *letting all things be* —
trusting only in the goodness
that *all* conditions offer me.
Liberate me from my holdings,
loosen me from 'knowing best'.
Let me rest in holy stillness,
softly in this letting-be-ness.

ANGELS, PRAYER AND NOW

It is clear that we live in a world filled with suffering. In some parts of the world, this is very obvious; in Australia, it's not so clear to some. Most of the world's population is hungry, while our society is overfed with high rates of anxiety and depression. In some countries, people suffer because their simplest living needs—food, clothing, shelter—are not even met. In other places, people work sixteen hours a day to pay for their cars, yachts, private jets and art collections. In the cities of less wealthy nations, people hang out for food. In the West, people hang out for the dealer, whether it's art or heroin. The Chinese ideogram for busy-ness is comprised of two elements: heart and killer. We all suffer in different ways.

What do people do with the leisure time they have saved? Leisure time for most people seems to be a void that demands to be filled by external stimulation; more videos have to be made, hired and watched. The very people who occupy leisure time have become the new celebrities. Actors, newsreaders, journalists fill our houses with their words and images. They tell us their version of how it is. They set up arguments between people who tell opposing stories of how it is. No-one need take the time to look around and observe. No-one ever has to sit in silence and ask why things might be the way they are. In fact, very few people seem to be able to bear leisure time. They have to do something; improve their minds; have to get those special, expensive shoes on and run around the cities. But even that is too silent, so they carry radios or talk into mobile phones as they jog.

They hire courts and bash balls at high speed or they drip over faxes in saunas or lie around and watch videos or they take drugs or alcohol to unwind from the above mentioned racing around. They wrestle together in athletic sex-a-thons. They do aerobics to make their bodies and hearts harder and harder. They shore up their rigidity.

I have started to come into some little understanding of what prayer means to me. It is not to ask for things, results or outcomes; even when these outcomes seem good to me. It is like trying to harness power to make things happen the way *I will* that they should. For me, to pray is to acknowledge that I simply don't know what is the best outcome for me or for another. I've never known and I never will. In my own lifetime some of the events that seemed tragic and fearful at the time, I now see were the beginnings of changes that are welcome and wonderful. Even so, these interpretations of welcome and wonderful are still only mine, judged by my relative self. I am incapable of seeing a bigger picture. These interpretations are not and never can be the truth, or the best. The most that can be said about them is that they are outcomes that please me. Whatever prayer is, it is most certainly not about self-interest.

PRAYER TO THE ANGEL OF NOW

All my lines are tangled, Angel,
see the mess projection makes!
Sharks of fear are tugging closer,
I'm caught off balance, my legs shake.
Help me withdraw all my harpoons
out of *what if, next year, when* . . .
Help me bring my scattered thinking
back to base where I can stand
safe and peaceful in the knowing
Now is all I need to have.
In this Now is all I need to live and love and breathe and be.
In this Now is all I want to let me live as truly me.

PRAYER AND AFFIRMATIONS

Nothing stays the same in this world of change. And it is the experience of this in my own lifetime that has led me to accept that the only prayer is one that asks for the grace and the courage and the love and the faith *to be with how things are*. My prayer is for *staying power with awareness*, rather than answers or solutions—although sometimes these occur in graceful ways.

I pray to have the courage to let go of controlling and planning and worrying and fighting to set up a future for myself that seems safe. There is no future in this world that is safe; the only way out of this world is through the chimneys. The sooner we become truly conscious of this fact, that no-one survives this world, the sooner that person's life—not to mention their prayers—becomes rich and real and, I should think, more fully lived, more fully experienced. Prayer is absolutely fresh and real; it can't be in the past or the future. Like an angel, a prayer can only be right now.

For me, prayer is the opposite of affirmations that people use in an attempt to change long-held attitudes or mental habits. There is no doubt that what we believe we are, is how we are and at this level, fighting thought with thought does work. Affirmations work because they are about this world and they are based in the business of this world. The same is true with 'prosperity' affirmations. Try it. You'll be surprised.

Anyone who has come to the place of prayer, however, has often tested all the things this world can offer. I have to say that there's nothing much I haven't tried; it was not my nature to leave doors unopened. The now discredited Bahgwan of the Rajneesh movement used to say, 'Go out and do it. Do sex and drugs and rock and roll. Do whatever you think will bring you peace and joy and happiness. When you finally find that nothing out there can do it, you will be ready to learn another way.' This was a wise teaching, it seems to me. By trying (and failing) to make something or someone in the world, events, situations, relationship with people, etc, work out as a person desires, the person can then come to a position of great truth; the truth of knowing that what they want cannot be satisfied, could never be satisfied, by anything this shape-changing world has to offer.

This can never be done by being preached at, but only by experience. As the great teacher Tara Singh puts it, a person finally comes to see that she has been wasting her mental and spiritual energy in 'the adoration of nothingness through which we perpetuate our torment'. We can adore nothingness in many ways. Whatever we invest soul energy in becomes god. That is how idols are made and worshipped; they are not just little figurines with emerald eyes. They can present themselves as the blessed trinity of ambition, promotion and success, or they can be a water-frontage four bedroom house, a secure future, education, physical health, beauty, a face-lift, true love, or indeed any 'self-improvement'.

PRAYER TO THE ANGEL OF BECOMING FULLY ALIVE

Wake me, Angel, from this trance.
This sleep walk, this sleep life
that I lead, day after day, so dull, so safe.
Neat in my home, neat in my job,
all things filed and sorted.
Every day a cup of tea at the same time,
same small talk. 'Fine, how are you? That's nice.'
Running on before they even answer because everyone
knows that it's only sleep talk. Ghost life. No life.
Angel, wake me from the spell of half life.
Crack thunder, flash light around me.
Prick the hairs on the back of my head with
some terrible visitation. Hurl me to the ground,
blind me with brilliance. Show me the face of love.

Let truth burst through me
Angel, help me now.

MYSTERY OF PRAYER

Prayer is not directed to the circle of self. It seems to me that it moves the prayer-maker into a different place in mind, an altered state if you like, because it breaks out of the treadmill of thoughts and the thinking of more thoughts. It breaks out—where? It leaves the ego system and who knows where it may travel? Into something greater?

What is prayer? What makes a prayer different from any other mind activity? For me, a prayer can be defined by asking as one can do with anything: what is it for? Prayer seems to be directed from the deepest part of individual self to something, some mystery apart from self; something greater than self in a mind movement that changes a singular experience into a universal one.

There are times when I've had to make a prayer out of what I had to hand in just the same way we learn to make a meal out of what's available in the kitchen, especially the night before pay day. I have had to make prayers out of the most intense, almost unbearable feelings of loss and desolation, because that's all I had. There was nothing else in me.

What changes these mere feelings into prayer, is the conscious decision to dedicate them in some way. In this way, any human experience can be made prayerful. Feelings of intense joy and delight can also be a prayer, an out-rushing of joyful energy. For me, the essence of prayer is its *mindfulness*, its consciousness, its decision to be dedicated and given.

There is a beauty and a dignity possible to the human spirit any time it raises its head no matter how beaten it may be feeling, no matter how appalling the surrounding circumstances, so that the spirit can say: 'This terrible desert is where I am; these desolate feelings are all I have. But I still have the dignity of choice and with this human facility I bring to mind all of us who are suffering like this anywhere in the world, and who have suffered like this and who will suffer like this.'

And this is my prayer, this fully alive sense of sorrow and

despair, joining with us all. It doesn't really matter to whom this is addressed, whether it's God, or Allah, or Jesus, or Buddha or Lord Krishna or the wisdom beings, or an angel, or the ancestors, or the Tao, or a more abstract version of Parent, or Universal Mind or just Other. What makes another ordinary instance of humdrum human suffering into a prayer is the mindfulness of the pray-er, the sense of dedication to, and the union *with*, rather than alienation from. Prayer is relationship in mind, bringing a sense of closeness with others. Prayer is communion. It is communion that is at the heart of the Christian ritual of worship.

PRAYER TO ROGER'S ANGEL

Help me, Angel, open to the flow
of all life's goods and riches.
To trust and touch the fullness of existence.
To live and feel the depth of all my feelings;
the force that makes me *me* and no-one else,
the strands that shape my own uniqueness

Take me deeper, Angel, wider,
take me lower, Angel, higher,
through the richness of my life
to breathe and sing, to swoop and swing
through breadth and width and depth and height
life's spiral dance, life's spice and bite.

PRAYER AND INNER PEACE

If a person starts to be aware of what's going on in her mind over just a few minutes or so, it can be pretty alarming. It can be something like Luna Park. Ferris wheels spinning around carrying memories of what I did last week, last year, twenty years ago; dodgem cars banging around in undecidedness, should I do this or should I do that; worries about what I should do next, next day, next year, going round and round; 'what ifs' whizzing through every possible outcome; chronic anxiety snaking around the ground; several dozen mind committees discussing whether or not I did the right thing last night, last week, last year. Or whether *they* did.

Crazy shooting galleries that knock down meaningless targets — only to have them pop up again. More committees debating, rehearsing what I might say, could say, should say, when I run into her again. What she ought to do; what they ought to do. The

Laughing Clowns never going anywhere, never saying anything, just turning their open mouths for the same old balls to drop in. The judgement committee arguing whether or not it was fair that this should have happened to me last week, last month, last year. Or to them. Or taking up some other long neglected case of gross injustice because the judgement committee never rests. It can always be relied on to dig up some old carrion to chew on.

The Ghost Train circles constantly, all those grinning skulls of old remorse, old shames, and regrets, round and round they go, disappearing for a while into the darkness, to emerge screaming out into the daylight again. All this feverish activity is going on and perhaps the person hasn't even got out of bed yet! That's how mad mind can be. This is where meditation can help; this is where a prayer can help.

A prayer, because it reaches out of Luna Park and into that other part of mind where depth and silence have their home, but which is rarely accessed because most of us stay in the fun fair most of the time; and meditation, because having found the place of stillness, mind seeks to rest there and the deadly obsessions of wild, undisciplined mind can release. A prayer can break through the craziness and intervene. With practice, the wheels slow down; the screaming fades; stillness can happen. Wild, undisciplined mind, where all suffering comes from, can be calmed. Continual practice brings more peace.

PRAYER TO THE ANGEL OF MIND

Angel of Mind, teach me how to rule my kingdom.
Teach me that what I dwell on will increase.
Teach me that what I let go will decrease.
That what I bind on earth will be bound in mind.
That what I loose on earth will be loosed in mind.
Teach me new, loose mind.
Show me kind, ungrasping mind,
soft, aware, accepting mind.
Mind that neither clutches nor rebuffs.
Mind that neither runs away nor chases.
Mind that grows and opens wide
to simply shine its nature
onto everything in Light,
onto everything in Love.
Teach me, Angel, Heaven's secret

so that I can share with all.
Mind and Love are both the same thing;
Mind and Love made out of God.

Because it is easier to start practising these disciplines of mind when one is still relatively comfortable, it is almost as if we, who are not this minute dying in a hospice, stupefied with narcotics, have a duty of care to those of us who are. We can start practising peaceful mind right now. These attitudes can be immensely powerful in ways we can't understand via the intellect. Any time is the perfect time to start practising letting go of fuelling the Thought Machine.

The Exodus journey has been likened by many wise people to the journey of each individual spirit. Prior to awakening, the spirit lives in slavery in Egypt, the land of the dead. There is food and shelter and security. But one is a slave. Whether a person is a slave to habitual, dispirited living, staying on in a hated job to pay a mortgage, or slave to addictions of some sort, or slave to compulsively needing the approval of other people, matters little. Staying with the known is staying in Egypt, living and dying a slave. But once the spirit has been wakened, it is no longer possible to remain in Egypt. The desert calls, with all its freedom and terror and with this call comes the invitation to trust in life and the processes of life, even in all the fear. In this situation is prayer then just a shoring up of trust when it falters? Praying in faith to have more faith?

As I grow older and move closer to the last part of my life, I'm coming to see that it is our deep, rich and vibrant relationships with each other that nourish and sustain. It is with and through prayer that I remember the truth of the connection between us all. Even those who seem far away from my life, my country and my way of being.

Connection, relationship, unity in difference, the harmony that can embrace Marian Woodman's 'tension of the opposites' in mind—these are the metaphors for living with responsible sensitivity to each other, the physical world and the graceful and wondrous non-humans who share the planet with us.

Angels bring 'tidings of comfort and joy'. Whether a person regards them as poetical fancy or as personal beings, doesn't really matter. In the long run, no one can ever know the truth about these matters. Prayer is thought. Thought is metaphor. All we can do is live.

PRAYER TO THE ANGEL OF STILLNESS

Fold me, Angel, in deep stillness.
Hold me in this silent place.
Unravel in me every teaching,
every 'truth' I've fought to hold.

Unwind all the world has taught me.
Shake loose every foolish thought.
Leave me emptied of my knowings
in the peace I've always sought.

Teach me all about allowing—
open handed to embrace.
Help me make the longest journey
from my smart brain to my heart.

PART THREE

Prayers

PRAYER TO THE ANGEL OF FULLNESS

Fill me, Angel, with your goodness,
Let me take in all that nurtures.
Let me take my time and savour
all the flavour, all the fullness.
Let my life be full of grace.

PRAYER TO THE ANGEL OF RELATIONSHIP

My mind has been split off from my heart,
seeing you as different and somehow *wrong*.
This must mean I am *right* and that you need correcting,
even punishing.
Angel, help me see that all my perceptions are so biased,
so contingent on what *I* want, what *I* feel, what *I* think . . .
that I can't really be trusted whenever I feel separate from heart.
Heart tells me we are all in this together.
Heart tells me I am just being silly when I want to be right.
Heart shows me how to throw back my head and laugh heartily
at this funny person wanting to be *right*!

PRAYER TO THE ANGEL OF TRANSITION (for any one of us in the place of change)

Hold me, Angel, in this shifting place.
Like ice floes breaking up or earth splitting open in a zig-zag crack,
this is the change to something else.
This is new river; this is new ground.

This is flash flood; this is no ground.
This is the swing bridge over the abyss with too many slats
missing and my feet skidding through to nothing.
I can't go back; the slats crumble behind me.
I can't go forward, there is only air.
This is the hell climb up the Eiger—fingers clutching stones
that break away;
I have nowhere to be. There is nowhere for me.

Terrible gears are grinding.
Dreadful fears unwinding.
This is the bardo, molten with demons.
Hold me while this change unfolds in me.
No-one here will help because the strongest accusation of the world's pointing finger is: *You have changed*.
Angel, help me.

PRAYER TO THE ANGEL OF FAMILY LOVE

Hold me, Angel Mother, in your warm wings.
Remind me of my place in Heaven
Restore me to the truth about myself:.;
I am not here to command or judge
but love.
Of course my child is different to myself
and lives his life in different ways than me.
Remind me of the deep respect of Heaven.
Remind me of the way I need to be.
Remind me of the way to love my mother.
Remind me of the open way of heart.
Fill any gap in time and space between us
with Heaven's flowing heart and welcome gates.
It doesn't really matter if she's in this world or not,
in Heaven all the worlds are safely kept.

What matters is the love between us all,
She and me and then my child
and all the children of this world.
One day we'll all go home together.
Until then, remind us of the truth.

PRAYER TO THE ANGEL OF BEING WRONG

Angel, teach me how to be wrong.
Teach me how to acknowledge my mistakes.
Teach me to let go of ego, puffed up pride
that says 'No, I didn't. And if I did it's your fault, never mine.'
Teach me how to make them welcome,
my mistakes, with grace.
Teach me to be wrong. Not in sulky saintliness.
Not in hurt withdrawal (reproachful eyes that say
'Look what you've done by thinking I was wrong.
How *could* you?').
But show me how to be vigorously and magnificently wrong,
thoroughly and utterly *wrong*.
No-leg-to-stand-on wrong.
Completely *wiped out wrong*, blown away wrong.
Taken to the cleaners wrong.

No-correspondence-entered-into *wrong*.
Fabulously, wildly and enormously WRONG!
Then teach me how to say all in good time:
'Forgive me, my companion. I was wrong.'

PRAYER TO THE ANGEL OF TRUE LOVE

Let me let my loved ones be themselves
Angel of Love.
Let me withdraw my judgement of *how they ought to be*.
My narrow little way of seeing is all about *me*.
What *I* think they should do,
what *I* need them to do,
what they should do that *I* approve of.
Angel, help me see that judgement is the worst of selfishness;
a self-obsession that others be clones of me.

Help me see the violence in this way of judging.
Help me see that it is based in hatred.
Hatred of their way of being. Hatred of their whole, true selves.
Release me.

Let me see that they are for themselves and for their God
and not to do with me at all.
They have their ways and lives and work to do. And so have I.
My own rich life will free me from the need to crucify.

PRAYER TO THE ANGEL WHO DEFENDS AGAINST CAT MIND

Holy Angel, holy Mind.
See what I'm doing. All my claws are out and I'm hanging on,
grasping with cat mind.
Wanting to be comfortable in the sunshine.
Wanting no disturbance. No growth. No movement.
Resisting change.
Just curled up in the sun. Purring in my sleep.
Dreaming of chewing tiny heads off birds.
Mousy victories. Batting a lizard's remnant.
Mighty cat hunter.
Dreaming I'm a cat when I am a child of God.
Help. Awaken my mind to the vastness of truth.
Open my mind to the surging of life.

PRAYER TO THE ANGEL OF SURRENDER

I come to you, exhausted by my struggle to manipulate,
coax, fight, argue.
I come to you at the end of my wits,
exhausted with trying to have my way.
I am finished.
I surrender.
I place the battle in your radiant hands.
I see you lift it up to be solved by a higher wisdom,
a wiser love than mine.

Now I feel the emptiness,
the loss of effort, the end of struggle.
Angel of surrender, be with me in the void.

PRAYER TO THE ANGEL OF THE SHADOW

Be with me in the darkness; I have fled you all my life.
For the first time I stay still.
Surrendered.
Shivering.
Empty.
Perhaps it is only the dark shadow of your wings
that gives depth, breadth and perspective to my being.
But I cannot yet—if ever—welcome the pain of that knowledge.
Angel of the Shadow,
be with me and help me not to run.

PRAYER TO THE ANGEL OF GRIEF AND LOSS

Be with me, Angel, in this grief that floods my heart,
that threatens to overwhelm me.
This ocean of stormy sorrow that has swamped my tiny craft and
threatens to wash me into depths I dare not think about,
let alone experience.
This sea of present sorrow seems to be fed as well
by rivers of old grief; old deaths and sorrows never fully mourned.
Poor unacknowledged ghosts of losses past still haunt me.
Sometimes my life seems made of loss and this is one such time.
Please hold me so I am not drowned,
dissolved,
annihilated by these feelings.
I am so little and this sorrow is enormous.
Just hold me.

PRAYER TO SANDI'S ANGEL

Angel, I don't understand the forces that threaten
to overwhelm me
in this time of deep and inwards change.
And all my life I've had to understand.
Help me see that this is not about understanding.
This is not about anything I know.
This is so hard for me, Angel, to be still and helpless
in the face of this anxiety.
To simply be and feel the painful feelings.
To simply be and let myself renew.
Hold me while these feelings flow through me.
Wrap your warm wings around me.
There is nothing I need do.
Keep me still.
Shelter me.
My own Angel, shield me while I grow.

PRAYER TO JEANETTE'S ANGEL

I turn to you, Angel. There is nowhere else to go
when I feel overwhelmed; at the mercy of my pain.
You saw my history being made; the suffering, the cruelty.
Why is it children suffer so?
And do their angels stand beside them helpless to defend?
These things are mysteries past my understanding.

And beyond my understanding is the peace I seek.

So I ask that you unfold your wings around me
And comfort me with soundless angel song.
Your covering wings press close about to warm me
and hold me, Angel, in this overwhelm.

PRAYER TO JOHN'S ANGEL

Hold me in the letting go
of everything I love and know.
Hold me in the packing up
and folding up of old, known self.
And help me in this steep descent
to deepest truth of truest Self.

Help me, Angel, while I move
from time's short forms to endless Love.

Angel, hold me through this night,
Angel, hold me till the Light.

PRAYER TO THE ANGEL OF DELIVERANCE
(For Philippa and all of us)

I'm doing it again, Angel.
Seeking the kingdom 'out there'.
Deliver me.
Chasing the world of ideas and cleverness like a silly puppy spinning round its tail.
Deliver me.
Running after Rich and Smart as if they were the truth.
Deliver me.
Looking for a big break that will make my reputation.
Trying to get my portrait painted for the Hall of Fame.
Yearning for a partner as if this would bring God.
Deliver me.
Lead me by the waters where my heart can sing in peace.
Lead me to the deeper stillness where my treasure is.

PRAYER TO THE ANGEL OF ENOUGHNESS (For Maggie)

Teach me, Angel, that what is in me is enough.
Whisper to me, Angel, that there is nothing else.
This person, this heart, this mind, this world, this life
are rich enough and deep enough for me.
Old conspirators, brain and ego, are always at it;
starting up another paper chase.
Gotta have this, gotta have that, gotta have him.
Then I'll be happy. Run and fetch it.
Run, run, run, away from Self,
away from Truth, away from Love.

Hurting myself in trying to find them out there where they *never* are.

Turn my footsteps home, Angel. Home to here.

Home to stillness.

Home to me.

Hold me close and wrap me in enough.

It is only in deep stillness that my treasure shows itself.

PRAYER TO MADELEINE'S ANGEL

Darling Angel, wrap me round
with mighty wings and angel song.
Sing me quiet and sing me calm,
sing me stillness in this storm.
Sing me of the peace of heaven,
sing me to the place of haven.

There I breathe and be in peace,
there all racing wild things cease.
Safely wrapped in angel wings,
myself the gift your soothing brings.

PRAYER TO SABINA'S ANGEL

I need you, Angel, to remind me in this world of busy noise
that heaven is just here, right there, if I can only stop and listen.
Find the silence, find the calm, find my stillness and my centre.
Ask your peaceful song to enter.

Hold me in my daily doings, so I stay
still and peaceful while I pray my prayers of shopping, cleaning,
sweeping, cooking; all the prayers a mother prays.
Let me know I must make time for me or I go mad
and have no time for others. And they are little for so short a while
although
sometimes it seems forever. They grow and go.
Teach me this and teach me love so I can also grow and go.

PRAYER TO THE ANGEL OF PEACE

(For Georgina)

Angel, you were there and saw
the madness of my early life. The whirl of passion, drama, pain.
I have had enough of strife. I seek the hush of sanctuary.
My soul has led me here to these vast gates where you wait to lead
me to the Garden.
But now I find new terror in this silence.
Now I find new monsters in the dusk.
Sometimes I think I will run mad in all this peace.

Help me, Angel, stay and learn and grow.
Curve your mighty wings of peace around me.
Raise your lamp and expel all my demons.
Then stand with me in this new place.
Stay with me on this untouched ground.

Help me blossom in the quiet.
Show me my true nature in the silence.
Pray with me where new life shoots; where new buds swell.
Help me find the greatest secret in the world;
what might arise in a mind now freed from other people's noise.

PRAYER TO THE ANGEL OF THE PEACEFUL WAY (For Virginia)

Angel of the Peaceful Way,
give me space and depth to play.
Give me freedom from my thoughts. They take me hostage, Angel.
They exploit me, manipulate me and punish me all my life:
That's no good, I'm no good, he's no good, I need this, I need that, I don't want this, I want that, get this, get that, have this, have that, rush and get it, step and fetch it. Hurry, hurry, God, you're hopeless ...
My thoughts are my enemies. They seem to hate me. Then they seek others to blame and ambush.
Release me, Angel, from their power.
Made in the War Room of a frightened child; dispatches for defence; the war has been over for fifty years and still they command *Attack*!

And I am the first in the line of fire.

What might happen, Angel, if their hostage got away? Walked away from these crazy battalions?

Tell them their whipping girl has gone AWOL—run away with an angel.

If they want war, they'll have to start without me.

Angel, let's go flying.

I will no longer live with insane thoughts but in the space of God.

PRAYER TO VENISE'S ANGEL

Angel, help me let him go,
this person that I love so much.
Take my hands and show me how
to loose my hold and let him be.

Let a wiser love than mine,
a deeper, truer love enfold him.
Help my sticky fingers loosen,
let him sink into the Truth.

Teach my heart that human love
is always dark and compromised.
Then may the love of heaven shine
through these open hands of mine . . .

PRAYER TO THE ANGEL OF THE SACRED TEMPLE

(a special prayer for women)

Once again I've done it, Angel. Taken my soul to the man
instead of to the temple, instead of to my holy place.
Wanting him to be God, to be my saviour.
Expecting him to heal my heart wound, cure my sorrow.
He quite gently has refused me; knows my soul is not his business.
Knows two souls is one too many for a human being to care for.
Now I am alone and hurting.
Only You can make it better, Mysterious Other deep within.

Show me how to shape devotion so that heart is soothed and calmed.
Show me where the deep maps in me chart the holy promised land.

PRAYER TO GABRIEL, HEAVEN'S MESSENGER

Gabriel, are there any messages for me?
Are there things that I should know? Something I could do that would bring peace?
Please tell me.
Are there people I could write to? People I could ring?
And is there something just for me to know?
A special knowing from the heart of Love?
A special thought to settle in my mind and bring me joy?
In silence and in certainty I wait to hear your voice.
In silence and in certainty I rest within your wings.

PRAYER TO THE ARCHANGEL MICHAEL

Protect me please, Michael, when darkness assails me.
When hell creatures taunt me
and I stand accused or accusing remind me,
we're all the same family.
Hear my prayer for the sick and suffering,
the hale and hearty, the brutal and beastly,
the sweet and the saintly, I pray for us all.
We're all the same people, all the same family.
Pray for us.
The murdered hostage and his killer,
I pray for them both and the man who gave the orders.
The bleeding woman and her rapist I pray for
and his mother, too, who taught him such hatred.
Stalin and Ghandi, St Francis and Hitler.
We're all the same family.
Pray for us.

PRAYER TO THE ANGEL OF THE TURNING POINT

Angel, I have had enough of suffering, grief and pain
and can no longer live like this with hatred, rage and blame.
Somewhere deep inside I know there must be another way,
so now I ask you help me find it please, today.

How things are in my life right now—
there's a swear word that says it all—
I have had enough; I can't take this anymore.
Please help me find the first step towards the new path that I need
to come to peace, to come to softness, perhaps one day, to joy.
Angel, can you help me? Can you find me my way home?

PRAYER TO THE ANGEL OF THE UNENDURABLE

No. This is too much. This can't be borne.
This is too terrible and I am crushed beneath its weight.
Why is it like this? Why do we live and love and lose
everything we hold so dear?
Why is it all taken away?
Who set it up like this?
Who made this up?
Where is the love in this?

There is no love in me now, just barrenness
and grief and pain and rage that it should be like this.
Angel, howl with me. Tear your hair.
This is the only prayer I can imagine
to howl in the horror of this desolate place,
dead seas and a grim moon.

PRAYER TO THE ANGEL OF THE TERRIBLE DAILINESS

Every day the same day, every day.
The to-ing and fro-ing, the leaving and coming home.
Rising, working, eating, sleeping.
Nothing changes; terrible dailiness, day after dreary day.
Angel, help me. Break into my safe.

This hard-cased mind only knows one way.
Show me another. Angel, crack this monkey-nut open.
Show me the seed
inside that can grow into the trees and flowers along the playful,
dancing, singing path where anything can happen.
Angel, make it happen. Make *me* happen.

PRAYER TO MARA'S ANGEL

When I pick up men to hurt me, Angel, don't leave me.
When I pick up drugs to harm me, Angel, stay close by me.
When I hate myself, please love me.
When I hurt myself, just hold me.

Angel, stay close by me
so that maybe one day
when I call out 'Help me, Angel'
someone will be there.

PRAYER TO THE ANGEL OF CHRISTMAS

Angel, you announce glad tidings.
Let them sink into my heart.
Joy to the world can't happen if I fail to play my part,
if I fail to love this self, this person God has caused to be,
this funny, tricky soul I live with—each hour, each day
this *me*!
At this time of family gatherings whisper to me.
How to honour all these people, all these souls surrounding me.
Teach me deep respect for little ones so that they in turn
may grow up with respect for all and peace can bless this world.
Dismantle in me, holy angel, the root of human pain;
insistence things be done *my* way.
Help me relinquish my self will, my urge to dominate.
Without such peace in families how can the world be saved?

Let my people be themselves without my interference
and teach me how to bless us all,
our different paths, our different ways.
And in this blessing given freely
my own release from self will come.

PRAYER TO MARGIE'S ANGEL

Angel, I lose touch with the very truth of me.
I lose myself in busy-ness and work and then
like someone waking up in a strange place, I look around and say
'Where am I? How did I get here?'
Remind me to stay close to my spirit, my inner home.
Remind me to visit often through the day,
no matter how busy, how rushed.
No matter how others are around me.
Remind me to take just a moment for myself, to breathe, to be,
To experience me.
Remind me that one day it all stops, the busy-ness and work
and all I will have then will be myself. Will I be famished,
fearful and neglected as I make the final journey?
Or rich and free and shooting like an arrow to the Mark?
As I hope to be then, help me be now, Angel,
and live each day with fullness, joyful on my path.